HISTORIC PHILADELPHIA

HISTORIC LANDMARKS

Jason Cooper

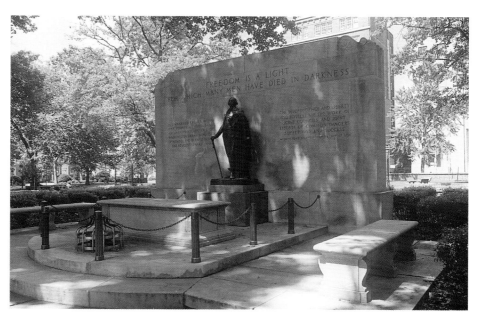

The Rourke Book Company, Inc.
Vero Beach, Florida 32964

PHOTO CREDITS:
All photos © James P. Rowan

PRODUCED & DESIGNED by East Coast Studios
eastcoaststudios.com

EDITORIAL SERVICES:
Janice L. Smith for Penworthy Learning Systems

Library of Congress Cataloging-in-Publication Data

Cooper, Jason, 1942-
   Historic Philadelphia / Jason Cooper.
      p. cm. — (Historic Landmarks)
   Includes index.
   ISBN 1-55916-326-7
    1. Historic sites—Pennsylvania—Philadelphia—Juvenile literature.
2. Philadelphia (Pa.)—History—Juvenile literature. [1. Philadelphia (Pa.)—History.
2. Historic sites.] I. Title.

F158.37 .C66 2000
974.8'11—dc21

                  00–038729

TABLE OF CONTENTS

HISTORIC PHILADELPHIA

Many cities brag about their place in American history. But no city has greater bragging rights than Philadelphia, Pennsylvania.

Philadelphia is sometimes called the Birthplace of the Nation. There's a great deal of truth to that nickname.

The two **documents** (DAH kyoo ments), or official papers, closest to the hearts of Americans were signed in Philadelphia. The Second Continental Congress **adopted** (uh DAHP ted) the Declaration of Independence on July 2, 1776, in Independence Hall.

Much of Philadelphia's history is protected in the many sites of Independence National Historical Park. This photo shows Independence Hall.

The Declaration basically said that the American colonies would no longer agree to the rule of England. Together, they would be a new nation.

In 1787 the Constitutional Convention also met in Independence Hall. The convention's work has become a monument to law and **democracy** (di MAH kruh see). The convention adopted the United States Constitution. This document promises Americans' rights and sets up the American system of government.

The Liberty Bell Pavilion is one of 24 sites within the historical park, operated by the U.S. National Park Service.

THE FOUNDING OF PHILADELPHIA

Swedes, in the 1640s, built the first permanent settlement in what is now Philadelphia. Later, settlers from Holland and England moved in. In 1674, England took control of the settlement. Soon after, a man named William Penn organized the colony of Pennsylvania. Penn chose Philadelphia as its capital.

The old City Tavern is one of the attractions in Independence National Historical Park.

Penn felt that everyone in Pennsylvania should have complete freedom of religion. Thousands of people flocked to Philadelphia from Europe. Some traveled to gain religious freedom. Others came to escape war, starvation, or **poverty** (PAH ver tee), the state of being poor.

By 1760, Philadelphia was a growing city of 20,000. Its location on the Delaware River had helped make it a major production and trade center. Philadelphia was wealthy, but not all the townsfolk were happy.

The first bank of the United States is another one of the sites in Independence National Historical Park.

The Thaddeus Kosciuszko National Monument preserves the house where Kosckiuszko stayed in 1797-1798. A volunteer from Poland, he was an American hero during the Revolutionary War.

St. Peters Episcopal Church is one of several historic churches in Philadelphia.

SEEDS OF REVOLUTION

Philadelphia in the mid-1700s was still part of a colony under the rule of Great Britain. Many of Great Britain's taxes and laws about trade angered Philadelphians. The British rules also angered others throughout the 13 colonies.

Philadelphia became a center for protest against the British. In 1774 the First Continental Congress met in Philadelphia's Carpenters' Hall. People sent to the Congress were **delegates** (DEL eh guts). The delegates came from other colonies. They spoke angrily about the British. War between the Americans and the British was nearing.

The First Continental Congress met here in Carpenters' Hall to decide a course of action for the 13 colonies in their feud with Great Britain.

In May, 1775, gun battles were fought between Americans and British soldiers in Massachusetts. Shortly afterward, the Second Continental Congress delegates gathered in Independence Hall. Their job was to make huge decisions about the future of the colonies. Their meetings resulted in the Declaration of Independence the following year.

The Second Continental Congress gathered here in Independence Hall and issued the Declaration of Independence.

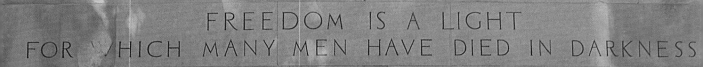

FREEDOM IS A LIGHT
FOR WHICH MANY MEN HAVE DIED IN DARKNESS

IN UNMARKED GRAVES WITHIN
THIS SQUARE LIE THOUSANDS
OF UNKNOWN SOLDIERS OF
WASHINGTON'S ARMY WHO DIED
OF WOUNDS AND SICKNESS DURING
THE REVOLUTIONARY WAR

THE INDEPENDENCE AND LIBERTY
YOU POSSESS ARE THE WORK OF
JOINT COUNCILS AND JOINT
EFFORTS OF COMMON DANGERS
SUFFERINGS AND SUCCESS.
WASHINGTON'S FAREWELL ADDRESS · SEPT. 17, 179

GEORGE WASHINGTON

BENEATH THIS STONE RESTS A
SOLDIER OF WASHINGTON'S ARMY
WHO DIED TO GIVE YOU LIBERTY

THE REVOLUTIONARY WAR

The Declaration of Independence made it official. The colonies would fight for their freedom.

The colonists chose Philadelphia as their capital. It remained their capital throughout much of the Revolutionary War (1775-1783). In September, 1777, however, the British Army defeated General George Washington's American Army at Brandywine, near Philadelphia. Washington's defeated soldiers spent the winter at Valley Forge, just 18 miles (29 kilometers) northwest of Philadelphia. The British Army spent the winter in Philadelphia.

The tomb of the Unknown Soldier of the American Revolution is in Philadelphia's Washington Square.

Meanwhile, France joined the Americans in fighting the British. In June, 1778, French warships threatened to trap the British in Philadelphia. The British Army retreated, leaving Philadelphia to the Americans.

Philadelphia's Fort Mifflin, now restored, took a pounding from British guns in 1777 and lay in ruins while the British moved into Philadelphia.

VISITING HISTORIC PHILADELPHIA

Today a visitor finds many historic buildings and neighborhoods in Philadelphia. Among the attractions are Independence Hall and the Liberty Bell. The bell was rung in 1776 to signal the colonies' independence. Visitors also enjoy Carpenters' Hall.

At Elfreth's Alley, visitors walk on a narrow, cobblestone street. It's one of the nation's oldest neighborhoods.

GLOSSARY

adopted (uh DAHP ted) — to accept formally and put into effect

delegate (DEL eh gut) — one who goes to a meeting as a representative of a group

democracy (di MAH kruh see) — the system of government in which the people vote to make decisions

document (DAH kyoo ment) — an official paper

poverty (PAH ver tee) — the state of being without; being poor

INDEX

FURTHER READING

Find out more about historic Philadelphia with these helpful books and information sites:

Knight, James E. *Seventh and Walnut: Life in Colonial Philadelphia*. Troll, 1999.

Steen, Sandra and Susan. *Independence Hall*. Silver Burdett, 1994.

Historic Philadelphia, Inc.
   historic.philly.com